SHOULDN'T ICE COLD BEER BE FROZEN?

My 365 Random Thoughts To Improve Your Life Not One Iota

By
Chris Gay

Suesea Press

Shouldn't Ice Cold Beer Be Frozen? My 365 Random Thoughts To Improve Your Life Not One Iota
Second Edition
Copyright © 2011 by Chris Gay

All Rights Reserved
No part of this book may be reproduced or transmitted in any form or by any means, including electronic or mechanical, including photocopying, recording, or by any information storage and retrieval system, without the written permission of the author.

Chris Gay
Suesea Press
Manchester, Connecticut
www.thepassionofthechris.com

Notice of Liability
The information in this book is distributed on a "as is" basis, without warranty. Although every precaution has been taken in the preparation of this book, Neither the author nor Suesea Press shall have any liability to any person or entity with respect to any loss or damage caused or alleged to be caused directly or indirectly by the content contained in this book.

ISBN 978-0-9844673-0-3

Dedication

This book is dedicated to me. However, I would like to take some time to thank all of those people who made such a tremendous impact on my writing career.
There…that ought to do it.

Also by Chris Gay

Humor:
And That's the Way It Was…Give or Take: A Daily Dose of My Radio Writings

Upcoming Fiction:
Ghost of a Chance

Introduction

Hi there, how are you? Well this seems kind of awkward. I mean, what do I say? I hardly know you. On the other hand you've bought my book and now out of some small sense of gratitude, I suppose I feel like I owe you at least a quick introduction before you dive head first into the comedy. What you'll find in the pages to follow is simply this: 365 Random Thoughts that have popped into my head at one time or another while I was busy writing historical comedy for the daily radio humor spots I broadcast in Connecticut. (You'll find that comedy published separately in my book And That's the Way It Was… Give or Take: A Daily Dose of My Radio Writings. Hey, do you like what I did there? I just totally, blatantly plugged my other humor book (so far) within the intro for this one) Anyway, what I've done here is bring together a compilation of my clever, witty, poignant, nostalgic and sarcastic takes on virtually every aspect of life, past and present. Have I succeeded? Well, if you've already paid for my book, it's a moot point as far as I'm concerned. If you're considering a purchase but haven't yet paid, I simply must ask-have you lost weight lately? Because you look fantastic! At any rate, let's get back to the topic at hand. So, you were browsing online or at your local bookstore; looking for something fun, yet thought provoking, to breeze through at the beach or, if you're in Indiana, at a lake somewhere. You wanted something that you can finish rather easily, and then feel better as you convince yourself that this counts just as much as reading a novel. Nice try. Though again, as long as you've purchased this book I really don't care. Who am I to judge you? So, now you'd like to jump ahead to the bite-sized, humorous morsels that I like to call Popcorn Humor, contained herein. But hello, what's this; an introduction? Hey, I know you don't want to waste time reading this part but admit it; you have just enough OCD in you to force yourself to continue on here. After all, we both know that you can't really lay claim to reading the entire book if you skip the intro, even in a book like this where said intro is wholly and completely unnecessary. For that very reason this introduction will go on, uninterrupted, for the next 72 pages. Just kidding. Go ahead, enjoy the book. We'll talk again at the Afterword.

"Either write something worth reading, or do something worth the writing."

—Ben Franklin

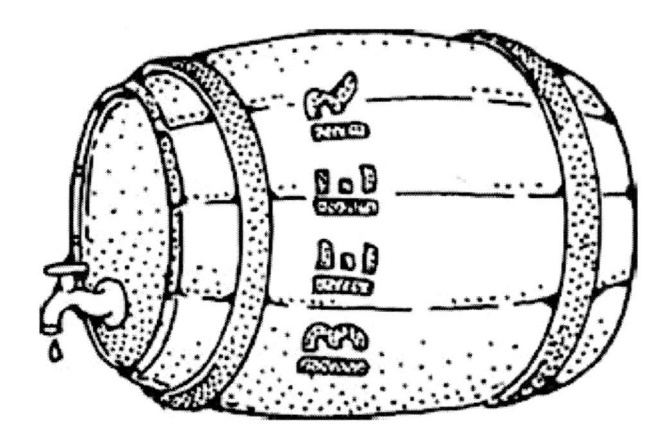

Shouldn't Ice Cold Beer Be Frozen?

1   Shouldn't ice cold beer be frozen?

ଽଓଔଷ

2   I'm guessing that Cap'n Crunch's military rank is really more of an honorary thing.

ଽଓଔଷ

3   When you open up a bag of peanuts and happen to catch the "Contains Nuts" warning on the label, whom do you tend to feel sorrier for in that instant; our legal system, or our society as a whole?

ଽଓଔଷ

4   Why does thinking about the *Jaws* theme while in a swimming pool still make you a little nervous?

5   How the hell were 15th Century cartographers so damn accurate?

ೞಡ

6   Admittedly, X does seem like the perfect letter to mark a spot.

ೞಡ

7   I wonder what the high school mascot is for the town of Climax, Michigan.

ೞಡ

8   I think now that someone has put a battery in a man's disposable razor, Schick and Bic have probably taken this battle a little too far.

Shouldn't Ice Cold Beer Be Frozen?

9 I wish that someone would invent a smoke alarm sensitive enough to be able to tell when it's just me cooking bacon.

ಬಿಲ್ಲ

10 Have you ever noticed that whenever you're running real early for something, the traffic lights you encounter on the way there are always green?

ಬಿಲ್ಲ

11 No offence to Sesame Street or PBS, but "The Count" has got to be one of the least intimidating vampires, like, ever.

ಬಿಲ್ಲ

12 Are TV weathermen who apply for jobs in San Diego really all that serious about their craft?

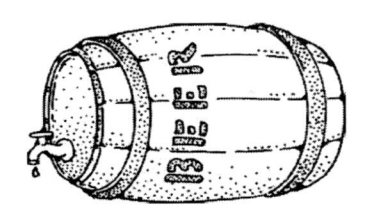

13 Why does Batman get to wear a fully armored suit while Robin only gets a pair of tights?

ଔଓ

14 With my luck, the story triumphantly touting the cure for death will appear in the same day's newspaper edition as my obituary.

ଔଓ

15 I wonder if hotels that purposely leave off the 13th floor for superstitious reasons realize that, nevertheless, the 14th floor is still the 13th.

ଔଓ

16 Who makes the decisions when radio stations run their *Memorial Day Top 500 Songs of the 1980's* feature? Is there really someone in the basement agonizing over whether *Sister Christian* or *Sunglasses at Night* deserves the rank of 184?

17   I still get a chuckle out of it whenever I see that scene in *The Towering Inferno* where O.J. Simpson saves a cat from a burning apartment.

18   Why is it so hard to bring yourself to disturb the pristine surface of a freshly opened jar of peanut butter?

19   I wonder how much the first guy ever to eat lobster got for winning the bet.

20   Even now without the Trans Fat, potato chips still don't seem all that great for you.

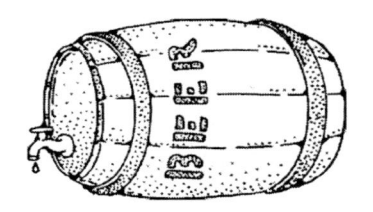

21 It's not bitching and moaning if your point is valid.

22 I've always been somewhat non-committal toward the whole concept of ambivalence.

23 Just once, for old time's sake, I'd like to call someone and get a busy signal.

24 At the end of *Terminator 2*, what were the odds that the bad terminator would be forced to drive a liquid nitrogen truck into a plant overrun with pools of white-hot liquid steel; the only two things on earth that could have possibly stopped him?

25   I would love to have a digital sundial.

ಬಂಡ

26   How come you never hear meteorologists say something like, "It's going to reach 97 degrees out there today, but with the Wind Chill Factor, it'll only feel like 89"?

ಬಂಡ

27   How is C-3P0 able to translate so much vocabulary for R2-D2 when all he emits are the same 8 beeps over and over again?

ಬಂಡ

28   In the movies, antique shop owners always seem to be up to no good.

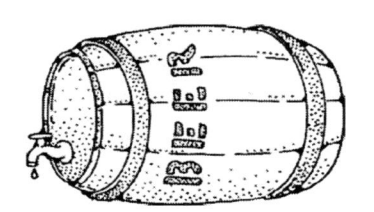

29   Why does Bruce Willis's wife leave him at the outset of each new *Die Hard* movie? Seriously, what does that guy have to do to prove he's a good catch?

ೞCಽ

30   When you think about it, the dumbest person you know knows more about medicine than most of the best Civil War era doctors.

ೞCಽ

31   Have you ever noticed how 49 degrees feels warm in March, but cold in September?

ೞCಽ

32   Pet Peeve: Eating jelly beans while watching TV with the lights off and deciding to take a chance that the dark bean is grape; only to find out instead that it's that horrific black licorice.

33   A friendly tip for the drivers representing the 207 up in Maine; that elongated vertical pedal near your right foot, if depressed farther down, will accelerate your vehicle to speeds in excess of 15 MPH.

34   The more I read *Dilbert*, the more I realize that Scott Adams is damn near spot on.

35   I've often thought it'd be wicked cool to have a Reverse Microwave; where you could get ice from water in, like, 20 seconds.

36   Of all people, why would SuperCuts have employed Terry Bradshaw as a spokesman? Were Mr. Clean and Ernst Stavro Blofeld unavailable?

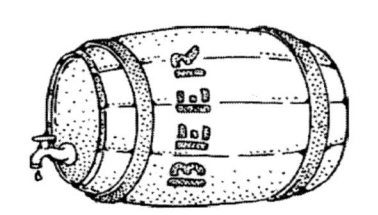

37 If the Freezing Point is 32 degrees Fahrenheit and 0 degrees Celsius, then why isn't it 32 degrees Celsius when it's 64 degrees Fahrenheit? You know, stuff like this is why I stick to writing.

ಬಲ

38 Although I love both the New York Giants and Buffalo Bills, I couldn't possibly care less what their official mustard is.

ಬಲ

39 I seem to be constantly at odds with the food industry as to what exactly constitutes a serving size.

ಬಲ

40 It appears that the age-old Tiffany/Debbie Gibson debate has finally cooled off a little.

41 When you see an advertisement for a comedian's upcoming show, why is his or her picture usually in black and white? I thought the whole point of their job was to be colorful.

ೞಛ

42 I've always been somewhat apprehensive with regard to electric toothbrushes. Plugging in an electrical appliance, only to then stick it into your wet mouth, just doesn't seem like the best of ideas.

ೞಛ

43 Pet Peeve: People reaching the front of a mile-long cafeteria line who simply must pay for their $6.89 lunch with exact change; while digging for so long into their pocket that Yale bestows an honorary Doctorate of Archeology on them.

ೞಛ

44 Do you know what's really difficult? Knowing just when to stop fast forwarding your DVR through the commercials while trying to get back to a TV special on the world's greatest commercials.

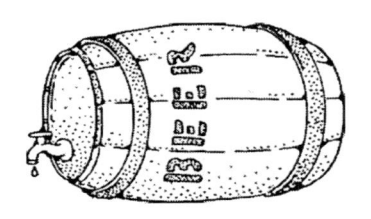

45   Whether you say the band's name R-E-O Speedwagon, or Reo Speedwagon, it still sounds kind of the same.

ঞ্চ

46   Why can't an expired driver's license be used at least for identification purposes; does your Date of Birth run out?

ঞ্চ

47   The fact that the famed London Bridge is now located in Lake Havesu City, Arizona still doesn't seem to take all that much away from the song.

ঞ্চ

48   With all of the riches, fame and notoriety of the Beatles, you'd think at some point someone or other would have pointed out the misspelling to them.

Shouldn't Ice Cold Beer Be Frozen?

49 In retrospect, the butler almost never does it.

ಜಡ

50 Last winter there was a crater in my gym's parking lot so big, I honestly think Neil Armstrong once referred to it as "Tranquility Base".

ಜಡ

51 Pet Peeve: If you get to the elevator and the door is more than halfway closed; let it go. Don't inconvenience the people already in there, you selfish bastard.

ಜಡ

52 I think Charlie Daniels was a little premature in declaring Johnny the winner in his contest with the devil. The devil went down to Georgia, all right; and got screwed out of his Golden Fiddle.

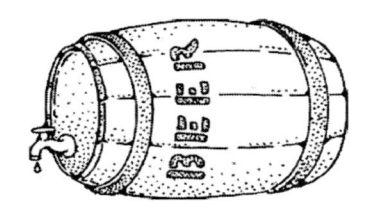

53   Why do all of the super-villains generally confine themselves to the one city that has a superhero? I mean, why didn't the Joker just leave Gotham City for, say, Chicago? Think of what he could have become in Omaha.

54   Are traffic signs that read *Right Turn On Red From Right Lane Only* really all that necessar? On second thought yeah, they probably are. Especially in Massachusetts.

55   Do you know what you'd miss much, much more than you'd think if it were suddenly gone forever? Catsup. Just try lasting a week without it.

56   If a Smurf kid didn't get what he wanted from his mom, did he threaten to hold his breath until he turned beige?

Shouldn't Ice Cold Beer Be Frozen?

57 There is nothing less temporary than a "temporary tax" placed on anything by any governing body that has the authority to do such a thing.

ଽଓଔ

58 If you couldn't feed Gremlins after midnight, how did you know when you could feed them again? Excepting one minute per day, it's always "after midnight."

ଽଓଔ

59 Why did the people who were always so concerned about dolphins being caught in tuna nets never seem to care all that much about the tuna being caught in them?

ଽଓଔ

60 Why do some crosswalks have signs in the middle of them that proclaim: *State Law Requires Motorists Yield To Pedestrians In Crosswalk*? In the absence of such a sign, does anyone really think they can mow someone down with a truck and then claim afterward, "Hey, what do you want from me? There was no sign."

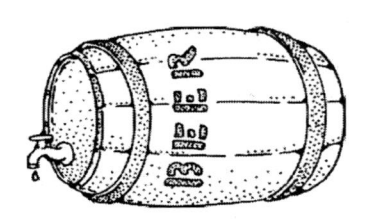

61 Pet Peeve: Heading out into a million acre parking lot that has only two cars still left in it; mine, and the one parked 6 inches from my driver's side door.

62 How long before months come with official sponsors; along with calendars printed with stuff like, *Miller Lite proudly presents- December?*

63 If the helmet worn by the dolphin in the Miami Dolphin's logo were to also have their logo on it, would the logo simply go on in perpetuity? Sort of like when you angle the bathroom mirror against the shower stall mirror and you see yourself, like, 4 million times?

64 Is there anything more oxymoronic than color-safe bleach?

Shouldn't Ice Cold Beer Be Frozen?

65 I've been wondering if the Capital Punishment statutes shouldn't be extended to include anyone who tosses his or her cigarette out of a car window.

66 Why on Wheel of Fortune, when the puzzle reads something like TH_ WIZARD OF OZ, does the contestant often say, "Pat, I'd like to buy a vowel. Is there an 'E'?" They should automatically lose their turn for stuff like that.

67 I wonder if Mick Jagger or Gene Simmons could get to the center of a Tootsie Pop in less than three licks.

68 Where does the pain disappear to during that 3 second gap between the time you stub your toe, and the time it finally arrives?

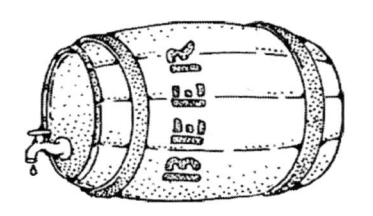

69   I'm guessing that every bachelor, at least once in his life, has tried to cook a turkey in a microwave.

70   The word Arid means dry. So essentially, the deodorant Arrid Extra Dry means Dry Extra Dry. Tossing in a repetitive consonant doesn't fool anyone, Arrid. I get it; you're dry.

71   Did the brain trust that gave Rhode Island its name just kind of hope that no one would notice that it is, well, not in any way whatsoever an island?

72   If they can install seatbelts in supermarket shopping carts, why can't they do it on bar stools?

Shouldn't Ice Cold Beer Be Frozen?

73 Christmas Eve really ought to be its own holiday.

74 I wonder if Aquaman is a vegetarian who refuses to eat seafood, but thinks eating meat is ok.

75 In TV commercials that feature couples, why is the guy half always portrayed as the idiot?

76 Though I'm not what almost anyone would consider religious, you ought to know that nowhere in our Constitution does it say that there is to be a separation of Church and State.

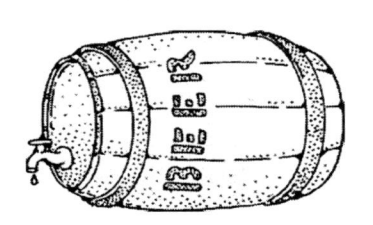

77 Statistically speaking, it's astonishing how often I am the millionth visitor to a given website.

78 I once started writing a humor book entitled *You Lost Me at Hello: The Female Guide to the Male Mind,* then stopped when I realized that there's not much of a market for a one page book.

79 During the 8 years of the Revolutionary War that George Washington spent being chased up and down the Eastern Seaboard by the British, I wonder if he ever stopped to ponder the phenomenal impact his heroic efforts would have on securing future Americans low interest automobile loans every February.

80 I once read a book where a *Jaws* actor challenged readers to try and tell the scenes with real shark footage apart from those that employed fake sharks. Ok well, here's my guess: the scene where Robert Shaw, as Quint, gets eaten alive by the Great White. I'll go with… fake shark. Final answer.

81 Why do foods without additives cost more? Apparently, we're being charged for subtractitives.

⊰⊱

82 Trust me on this: with regard to wristwatches, there is a definite difference between waterproof and water resistant.

⊰⊱

83 Ever notice how cool it is to say Wisconsin? I mean, if you pronounce it Wiss-consin…Go ahead, try it. I'll wait.

⊰⊱

84 Even after they were told it had happened and what to expect, why couldn't the Titanic passengers believe a severe gash below the waterline would sink the ship? The Titanic was huge, certainly; but it was floating in the Atlantic Ocean.

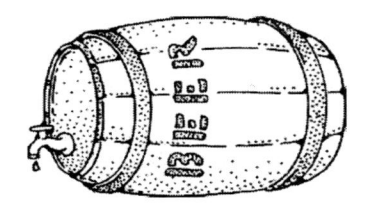

85 Why do hardcover books decrease in value faster than a 1988 Yugo with a manual transmission? They come out at $29.95; you turn your back for a second and for some reason it now costs more for the paperback.

86 Ringo got to sing lead on so few Beatles songs; why would he waste one on *Octopus's Garden*? Even that guy from The Eagles got to sing *I Can't Tell You Why*.

87 I'd like to think that if I suddenly found myself being tailgated by a speeding ambulance with sirens wailing, I'd be able to recognize it for what it was. Regardless of whether or not the word *Ambulance* was spelled backward.

88 A tip for the ladies: If you meet a guy at the gym or a bagel shop and you yourself start up a long conversation, try not to wait until you're 45 minutes in before you toss out a statement like: "You don't like broccoli casserole? That's so funny; my boyfriend doesn't either!" As a general rule of common courtesy, generic boyfriend disclosure statements should be made within the first two to three minutes.

Shouldn't Ice Cold Beer Be Frozen?

89 Just out of curiosity, I wonder what percentage of consumers heed the *Do not use in ear canal* warning on a package of Q-Tips.

ಸಂಬಂ

90 How come people will watch a movie on TV-and sit through all of the many commercials-when they have the same movie in DVD form sitting on their living room shelf?

ಸಂಬಂ

91 Seriously; does any person on Earth actually know the total number of timeouts per game an NBA or college basketball team gets to call?

ಸಂಬಂ

92 Why do so many of us native New Englanders consistently react to a forecast of snow as if we all grew up in Albuquerque, New Mexico? If we're to get 2-6 inches, bread and water will still be available tomorrow. What's worse is that we already know this; yet go through it every single year.

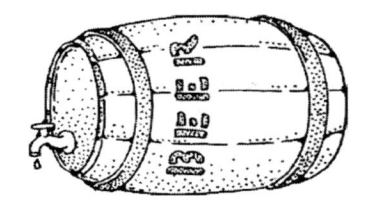

93 Did the television censors of the 1950's really think they were actually fooling anyone when they required that married sitcom characters sleep in separated twin beds?

ಬಂ

94 It seems it'd be much cheaper and almost as effective to simply buy and utilize stickers bearing the name of a home security company, rather than to purchase the actual security system itself.

ಬಂ

95 Why did it take the Post Office so long to come up with self-adhesive postage stamps? Those things should've been out by the 1960's.

ಬಂ

96 Here's a helpful cleaning tip: Use grape juice to remove club soda stains.

97 I've worked out in health clubs with *No Diving* signs posted on the wall next to the whirlpool. You know, whatever hope there is left for us just has got to be hanging by a thread.

ಜಂಥ

98 Did you ever wash your hands with an antibacterial soap advertising that it kills 99.9% of germs, and then wonder whether that last tenth of a germ would be the one that gets you?

ಜಂಥ

99 Voice actor Thurl Ravenscroft sang the original version of *You're a mean one, Mr. Grinch* and was also the voice of *Tony the Tiger*. Now, you'll never be able to hear one cartoon icon without thinking of the other. I hope that doesn't piss you off; but hey, what's done is done.

ಜಂಥ

100 Why is the volume that accompanies the presentation of the THX logo at the beginning of the DVD movies that feature it so absurdly out of proportion with the volume of the rest of the movie?

101 Have you ever looked down, noticed the Wash, Rinse, Repeat directions on a bottle of shampoo and wondered if, by comparison to the majority, you were smarter than you had originally thought?

☙❦

102 Why do they give you a receipt when you get a haircut? Is it even possible to get your hair refunded?

☙❦

103 "Those who would sacrifice liberty for a little temporary safety deserve neither liberty, nor safety." That is a Random Thought, I suppose; but it's not mine. It's Benjamin Franklin's. We can still learn a lot from our elders.

☙❦

104 I broke open a fortune cookie once to reveal a fortune that read, *Exciting new romance and great monetary success awaits you; so long as this cookie remains intact.* True story; in an entirely fictitious sort of way.

105 How did the Charlie Brown characters become so smart and philosophical at such a young age when all of their teachers spoke in an indecipherable, alien dialect?

ಸಿಐ

106 I wonder how long it'll take the PC crowd here in New England to try and change the term for blizzard from *Nor'Easter* to *Nor'Holiday*.

ಸಿಐ

107 What, I wonder, is the percentage of people who are actually laughing out loud as they text LOL?

ಸಿಐ

108 Do you really want to lose weight? Buy only unshelled nuts. The harder you have to work to get at that damn walnut meat, the more likely you are to give up after only a few.

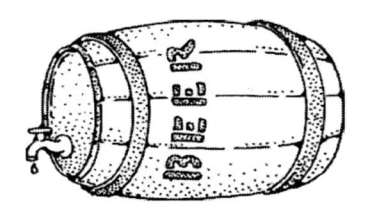

109 If a product is advertised for years as being better than the leading brand, then why isn't that product ever the leading brand?

※

110 Before they committed to calling themselves the *Los Angeles Angels* again, didn't anyone realize that that translates to the *Angels Angels*? Even I knew this; and I took French in high school.

※

111 I've invented a new word: Cartigo, Similar to vertigo, it's the sensation you get when you're stopped at a light with your brakes fully applied, yet still feel like you're slowly rolling backward; because the car next to you is rolling forward.

※

112 Do people who hit the automatic bathroom door opener to avoid touching the door handle not realize that they, along with many others, are still all touching the automatic bathroom door opener?

113   Being ambidextrous hasn't turned out to be quite as lucrative as I thought it might.

114   How many people who write *wish you were here* on a post card do you think actually do?

115   Someday, I'm going to write the story of how I made my first hundred bucks by the age of 30.

116   Just once, I wish Scooby Doo would have let Scrappy Doo fight the monster. Then, when he inevitably got his ass kicked, we'd have been done with him.

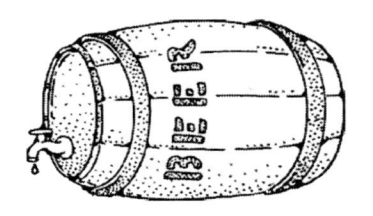

117   I'd really love to have a built in GPS for my car keys. That way I could hear something like, "Turn right in 3 feet. Lift up couch cushion and arrive at destination."

118   Why do some people refer to men in their late 50's as middle-aged? Do they expect that the majority of them will make it to 118?

119   Why did it seem that, though he kept getting older while taking progressively worse beatings, Rocky got smarter?

120   After seeing those jewelry commercials again this year, I'm reminded how hard it is to believe that a husband would give his wife a diamond on Christmas morning, while standing in their own living room, in front of their own tree, and say to her, "Happy Holidays, Honey."

Shouldn't Ice Cold Beer Be Frozen?

121 I'm getting tired of seeing the word reboot used as a verb in every 4th article I read on anything; especially in movie reviews of remakes. Endgame needs to go, too.

122 Why do so many gas stations put the fuel grade numbers out of sequential order? I think that they're hoping you won't pay attention and accidentally buy super premium instead of 87 Grade.

123 Who determined which months got an extra day or two? I'm thinking February really should have hired the July lobbyists.

124 Why do credit card companies put your replacement cards in the plainest white envelopes they can find; envelopes so distinguishable from every other kind you might receive that they can't help but get noticed?

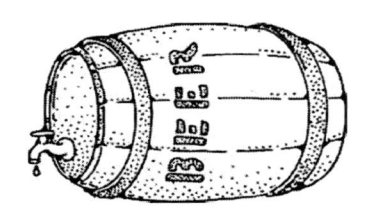

125 What's the point of banning smoking from buildings if you're still made to run past the gauntlet of smokers huddled together; vigorously puffing away two feet from the entrance?

ಬಿಐ

126 When I was a little kid and spotted a WRONG WAY sign while being driven somewhere by an adult, I always wondered how the sign knew where I was going.

ಬಿಐ

127 Why is it that we hear the most calls for lifestyle and energy conservation from people whose butlers take chartered flights to grocery shop?

ಬಿಐ

128 Whenever I have to spell out a word that includes the letter X, I always enjoy saying, "That's 'X'- like in "Xylophone," and then listening to the resulting confused silence.

129 I've nicknamed my driver *The Divining Rod*, because wherever I swing it on the golf course, it always finds water. It sits in the bag next to my pitching wedge; known as *The Desert Fox*, for its own special talent for finding sand.

130 As some coupons state that they have a cash value of 1/32 of a cent, have you ever been tempted to save up 3,200 of them, bring them to your local fast food place, and see if you can buy a burger off of their dollar menu? No? Me neither.

131 Soccer might be more fun to watch if every player except the goalie could use his hands.

132 Are television play-by-play announcers for sporting events necessary? "Johnson drops back to pass…" Really? You don't say.

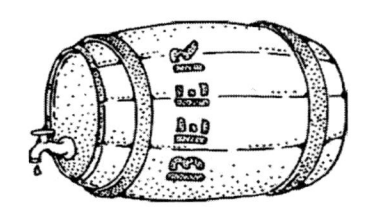

133 Why, when you're trying to turn into oncoming traffic, does every car speed by you-except for the last one-which goes just slow enough so that the others behind it can close the gap and catch up?

ಶ್ರೀ

134 Baseball Old Timer's Days are popular, but I think it would be more fun to watch a football version.

ಶ್ರೀ

135 Whenever I've had occasion to use a public clothes dryer, I can always tell if the person who used it ahead of me was a man or a woman simply by virtue of whether or not the lint trap was cleaned out.

ಶ್ರೀ

136 The times you live in don't feel like history while you're living through them, but they inevitably become history, notwithstanding. So pay attention...

Shouldn't Ice Cold Beer Be Frozen?

137 I wonder if the British have a harder time learning to drive a standard shift from the opposite driver's seat, as 85% of them are as right-handed as we are.

138 There are few tasks more depressing than taking down the Christmas tree.

139 That boulder chasing Indiana Jones in the opening scenes of *Raiders of the Lost Arc* seemed, well, almost comically round for a rock.

140 It's amazing how quickly Political Correctness progressed from silly to ridiculous to hypocritical to dangerous.

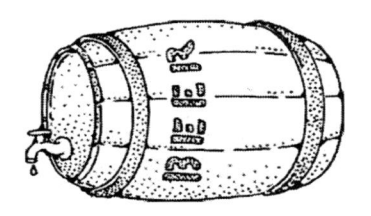

141 I'm kind of glad to see that there are still a few One Hour Photo places still around. You hang in there, guys. I'm sure film will come back into fashion once this digital camera fad fades away.

ಬಿಂಶ

142 Are tying shoelaces such a demanding chore that so many sneakers need to be equipped with Velcro?

ಬಿಂಶ

143 It appears that even a minor fracture sustained while playing ice hockey will not keep the doctor away; regardless of whether or not you've had an apple that day.

ಬಿಂಶ

144 The Milkman concept should be brought back into society. Only this time he'd also drop off things like vodka and rum. He'd be sort of like a Santa Claus for adults.

Shouldn't Ice Cold Beer Be Frozen?

145 I've always thought that a cute nickname for music dubbed *Soft Rock* would be Talc.

146 There are few greater, more compelling stories than that of the American Revolution and how our great country came to be. Perhaps someday they'll teach it once again in our schools.

147 It seems odd that dollar stores put circulars in the Sunday paper. I imagine a lot of weekly conversations that go something like this: "Honey, are there any dollar store specials this week?" "There sure are, Sweetie. In fact, while going through their flyer I noticed a bunch of items for only a dollar!"

148 Why didn't the rest of the characters in the movie *Groundhog Day* realize that they, too, were living the same day over and over again?

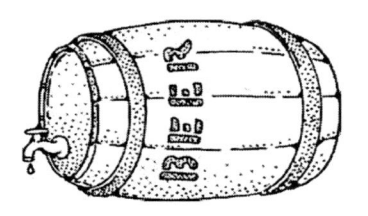

149 Why would anyone run from a ghost? Has any death certificate in recorded history ever listed "Ghost" as the cause of death? If you see one, chat a while. You'll never get a better chance to find out what's on the other side.

༺༻

150 Though they wear an absurd amount of armor, it almost seems like you can take out a Star Wars storm trooper with a Whiffle Ball bat.

༺༻

151 Sometimes squirrels remind me of soccer goalies, the way they stand perfectly still in the road, then suddenly dive indiscriminately to either their left or right.

༺༻

152 If you're over the age of nine, no group of chain restaurant employees should ever be singing some cheesy birthday song to you.

153 I wonder what motivation dolphins have for protecting us humans from sharks. I guess maybe they're paying us back for that whole albacore tuna thing.

154 Pet Peeve: Groups of three people walking horizontally through a 5- foot wide cafeteria hallway at the Speed of Tortoise.

155 Why can't a cursive N have one hump and a cursive M have two, like their non-cursive counterparts? This is simply another example of making life more difficult than it needs to be.

156 Though they never really get to see an actual live Saturday Night Live episode, Oregon residents seemed to have put it behind them.

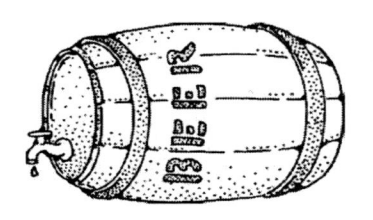

157 Clementines are everything oranges should be; smaller, seedless, tastier, and much easier to peel. So... why keep growing oranges?

ಸಿಂಜ

158 Could it be that now, with cameras starting to appear on Good Will donation boxes, the country has shed whatever remnants of the *Leave it to Beaver* era were left… forever?

ಸಿಂಜ

159 Have you ever noticed that the very young and very old almost always round their age up a year; as if it's some sort of achievement? The rest of us though generally cling to what we're at until the last possible second. I've heard people call themselves 8 1/2 and 89 1/2. No one is 46 1/2.

ಸಿಂಜ

160 Once, while tubing down the Farmington River in Connecticut, my inner tube was capsized in some rapids by a rock I could only assume was the namesake of Boulder, Colorado.

161 So, what is your disposition if you believe your glass to be one-third empty?

ಐಂ

162 Why does it seem that the loudest cries for "tolerance" and "diversity" come from the people, organizations and public figures that are the least tolerant of those who don't share their views?

ಐಂ

163 In your entire life, have you ever seen two burly guys carrying an absurdly large pane of glass down the street; except in the movies right before someone crashes through one?

ಐಂ

164 Listening to the radio the other day, I was surprised to find out there's actually an acoustic version of AC/DC's *You Shook Me All Night Long*. Who would've thought?

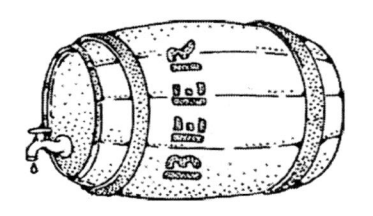

165 I would love to see how the inside of an igloo is furnished.

166 If you really think about it, pepperoni pizza is a perfect representation of the four food groups.

167 Why do snooze alarms give you an extra 9 minutes? That seems like such an arbitrary number. I can only assume that the feature was invented by Roger Maris or Gordie Howe. Or maybe the industry is just trying to screw with us. Or maybe it's because it's now 3:41a.m., and that's always around the time that thoughts like this occur to people.

168 I'm well aware that those individual cellophane wrapped slices of cheese food don't require refrigeration, but I'd be lying if I said I didn't I refrigerate them, anyway. Just in case.

169   How did Huey Lewis-in 1985-manage to get a song with the suggestive lyrics of *The Power of Love* into a movie like *Back to the Future*?

170   What's the point of alcohol-free mouth wash? I don't want to injure the germs; I want to wipe them out.

171   Do you ever find yourself giving consistently unfunny comics just "one more chance" day in and day out in the hope that just once the strip will pay off with a little humor; thereby justifying your continued loyalty to it?

172   It appears Will Smith has finally gotten the last laugh after taking second billing to DJ Jazzy Jeff for so long throughout the early years.

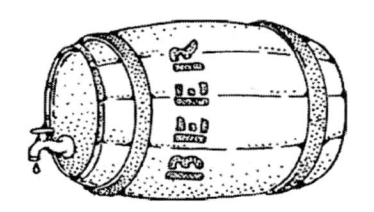

173   Why at a funeral does someone always say, "go on living your life, he'd want it that way"? Screw that. When I die, you damn well better believe I want everybody to never, ever stop grieving. And I'd want my girlfriend/fiancée/wife to join a convent.

174   Although I'm someone who greatly appreciates proper grammar, I can't help but love the cute way the Toronto Maple Leafs intentionally misuse it.

175   I wonder how many accidents were actually avoided due to those suction cupped "Baby On Board" signs in the 1980's?

176   Go over Niagara Falls in a barrel? Of Jack Daniels, maybe.

177   Pulling into a parking lot while blaring *Duran Duran* through your car's speaker system apparently doesn't make you look as cool as you might think. Or so I've heard.

178   A news story is only as big or small as it is allowed to be, based on the coverage given it by the major media outlets

179   I wonder what the elevator music version of songs from this era will sound like in 40 years. Perhaps the Eminem catalogue, as interpreted on the clarinet, will turn out better than one anticipates.

180   One of the reasons true racial harmony is so tough to achieve in America is because such an achievement would put so many media savvy race-baiters, of every color and political persuasion, on the unemployment line.

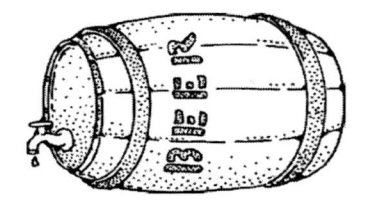

181 Whose ego is so fragile that there needs to be a 5 stroke limit in miniature golf? If people can achieve par on a Par 4, 410 yard hole in real golf, why should they get an extra stroke just to putt 30 feet; simply because they might have to avoid a toy windmill?

182 Why do Eskimos need 37 different words for snow? Is some snow colder than other snow? Is some snow made with Poland Spring? What I'm saying is, why confuse the issue?

183 Alaska and Hawaii were both admitted to the union in 1959, but Hawaii was last. If the order were reversed, would they have called the show Hawaii 4-9, or just dropped the concept all together?

184 I don't mind if we keep telling the World that we won't be bullied into using the Metric System; but I don't think the World will take us seriously until we replace two liters soda bottles with half gallon versions.

185   If someone had forgotten to italicize the period at the end of a sentence, the rest of which they had italicized, could you even really tell?

186   So, I'm expected to believe that St. Nicholas made it from the 4th Century until 1939 with zero sleighing issues and then, suddenly, his only way to combat heavy snow was to employ a 9th reindeer sporting a 75-watt red nose? I have to tell you; I remain skeptical.

187   Upon dating someone new, have you ever found yourself hoping he or she has the same cell phone provider as you; just so those 6 hour requisite "getting to know you" conversations aren't counted against your premium minutes?

188   With all of the possible names to choose from, we couldn't do better than naming the state below North Dakota, South Dakota? Yes, I realize that one is south of the other; but do you know what we call South Georgia? Florida.

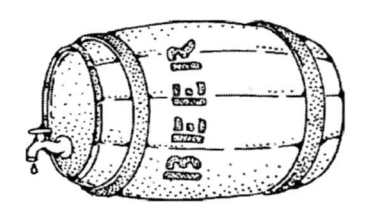

189 Cruise ships that fill their on-board pools with seawater are missing the point. If I had wanted to swim in the ocean, I'd have jumped overboard.

190 Every once in awhile I give a dollar to one of those charities that camp out in front of a supermarket, with the hope of getting a much larger positive karmic payback in return. So far, nothing. It's like the gods aren't even trying.

191 Some of the most intense and believable movie scenes take you out of the moment when a character rattles off one of those fake phone numbers with the 555 telephone prefix. My friends, the time has now come to take on this hot button issue and let Hollywood use a different nonexistent telephone prefix.

192 We're kidding ourselves if we think that there's an eighty cent flavor difference between 2 liter bottles of name brand soda and the generic store brand.

Shouldn't Ice Cold Beer Be Frozen?

193 Sorry Popeye; I don't buy that spinach routine. You would have made a great D H.

194 Why is it that your willingness to laugh at a bad sense of humor goes up in direct proportion to how attractive the woman who displays it is?

195 I know they're pretty convenient, but listening to books on tape still kind of feels like you're cheating.

196 I still cannot grasp that wrinkles would be such a problem that people would voluntarily utilize Botulism to combat them.

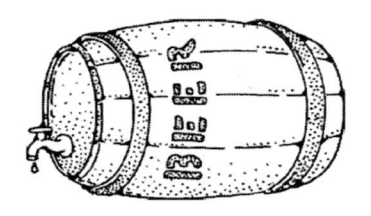

197 How do vampires manage to dress so impeccably, and without a hair out of place, when not a single one can see himself in a mirror?

༄༅

198 When you're born a Jr., does that suffix automatically become The II if you give your son your name? What if you never have a son; can you just call yourself John Smith II?

༄༅

199 I wonder if the real life office managers who laugh as they watch the movie *Office Space* even recognize themselves as the ones being parodied. From my experience, I'm guessing…no.

༄༅

200 Few things are more frustrating than being stuck on a two lane highway behind multiple 18-Wheelers that spend hundreds of miles trying to pass each other.

201   This country needs to put a much higher priority on bringing my Hartford Whalers back to Connecticut.

202   Have you ever dialed 867-5309 with random area codes just so you could ask to speak with "Jenny"? No? Me neither.

203   Have you ever bought a *Classic Rock of the '70's* compilation CD whose low price seemed too good to be true, only to later discover- after throwing away the receipt- that all the songs are covers performed by some no-name band with some no-name singer? No? Me neither.

204   I wonder what ice hockey and football players think when they read that some baseball pitcher will miss two weeks with a blister.

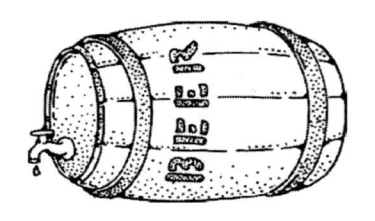

205 Pet Peeve: Friends or family who call you to ask for information, then when you start to tell them, they interrupt you to say they have to go find a pen. Have it ready when you call, nimrod.

206 It appears that rarely is there any middle ground concerning the looks of natural redheads; one way or the other.

207 I can't help wondering if the candy industry is behind the pushback of Daylight Savings Time until after Halloween.

208 It is unfortunate that the good majority of our country has never experienced the awesome seasonal changes we get to have here in New England.

209   I wonder if they'll ever invent sugar and rubber dispensing cigarettes to help people kick the chewing gum habit.

210   Why can aspirin company surveys always seem to find 4 doctors to recommend their product, but never get the 5th one to play ball?

211   Pet Peeve: When you're watching TV and a commercial comes on for some great looking new fast food product that's put out by a restaurant whose nearest location is 4 states away.

212   Sometimes I wonder if the only reason Thanksgiving was made a national holiday was to remind America that the Detroit Lions still exist.

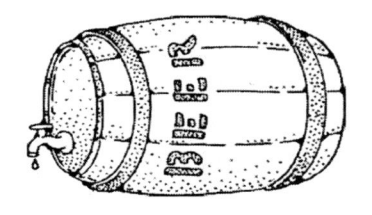

213 Ah, New Jersey, New Jersey, New Jersey. Garden State? Nice Try.

214 I wonder why you never see anyone out Trick or Treating dressed as Santa Claus. Now that would be showing a little creativity.

215 It seems like inflation has affected everything on Earth except the Ginsu knife. After 30 years, it still sells for only $19.99.

216 Why in most hotels are the ice makers and soda vending machines on alternate floors? That's like putting the washers on one floor, and the dryers on another.

217 Why does it feel that after centuries of comparatively small technological advancements, someone somewhere threw a switch in the 1940's that can't be turned off? Everything now is either vastly improved or obsolete within ten minutes.

ಬಂಬ

218 I still get chills when I think about the 1980 *Miracle on Ice* game.

ಬಂಬ

219 Have you ever pulled into a glorified fast food restaurant and noticed that they had valet parking? That's kind of like a liquor store handing out brandy snifters with the purchase of a six pack.

ಬಂಬ

220 It's interesting how fish never get suspicious of an earth worm, complete with protruding metal hook, just floating there suspended in place in the middle of a pond.

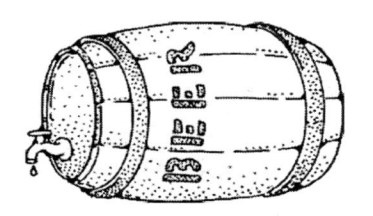

221   I'm curious as to why so few people outside of Connecticut know what a grinder is; yet for some reason I still know what heroes, hoagies, po'boys and subs are.

☙❧

222   Lance Armstrong was tested 7 times, and Big Bird not once? If after 40 years he's still the only one who can see "Snuffleupogus", should he really be on Sesame Street? Who steps in when he's on vacation? Cheech Marin?

☙❧

223   I wonder if Shirley Temple has spent her entire adult life dealing with dumb jokes from bartenders every time she's opted to order an alcoholic beverage.

☙❧

224   It now appears that I've spent my entire life believing that I was a Cancer when, in actuality, I may have been a Gemini. Not that I don't prefer Twins to Crabs, it's just that there ought to be some Department of Reimbursement created to handle refunds for the countless Cancer mugs and key chains I've bought throughout the years.

225 Participating in one of those family Christmas gift exchanges, where names are drawn out of a hat, is a little risky. It's kind of like asking your girlfriend if she wouldn't mind renting you a Clint Eastwood movie, without specifying which one. Sure, she might come back with *Dirty Harry*; but there's also a chance you'll end up with The *Bridges of Madison County*.

226 Why, when it comes to affairs of the heart, do you ask your close friends for their opinion when you know damn well that no matter what they tell you, you're still going to do whatever you planned on doing before you asked them?

227 It goes without saying that as a humor writer from Hartford, Connecticut, I've always loved Mark Twain. Yet, I can't help but wonder why anyone would bother going through the trouble of establishing a pseudonym if they were then just going to tell the world their real name, anyway.

228 Why didn't Captain America give himself a higher rank? Lieutenant Colonel America, at the very least. If he's partial to the Navy, Admiral America certainly has a nice ring to it. I mean, Hawkeye Pierce was a captain.

229 I'm still undecided as to whether it would be cool or weird if real life came with a laugh track; where every time you made a relatively nondescript wise crack, you'd be suddenly showered with laughter from a disembodied, non-existent audience.

230 I would love to be at a bank one day when some lottery winner goes in to cash one of those ridiculously oversized 3x5 foot checks they give them.

231 Though I was never in the military, I think the time they keep is so cool. Imagine if civilians used it, too: "Where? All right. We'll rendezvous at Starbuck's. 1300 hours, sharp."

232 Pet Peeve: Children of known actors who simply change their last names, get roles, and then say their lineage had nothing to do with it. Yes, I'm sure that topic never came up on a casting call.

233 When people opine that if you buy bottled water at $3 per you have no reason to complain about the price of gas, do they realize you're not required to fill yourself up with 12 gallons of bottled water every four days?

ಜಿಂಡ

234 How do cricket stand-up comedians know if their routine is going well?

ಜಿಂಡ

235 Life is way too short. A cliché, you say? Of course -but chances are you'll be lucky to be remembered at all past your own grandchildren. Think I exaggerate? Tell me, what was your own great-grandfather's birthday?

ಜಿಂಡ

236 It's awesome that even well over a decade after Charles Schulz passed away, most daily newspapers still run his *Peanuts* comic strip.

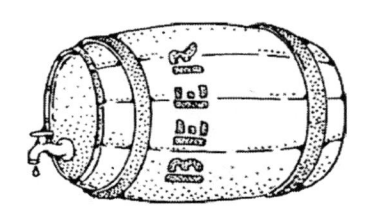

237 Those who moan about Christmas decorations staying up too late should consider examining what's really bothering them. Are people really chomping at the bit to get past the celebratory mood of December and into the utter elation that's brought annually with the coming of…January, February and March?

238 How did professional hockey go 50 years without goalies wearing headgear of any kind? You'd need balls of brass to stand tall and cut down the angle on a Bobby Hull slap shot, while wearing nothing on your head but a crew cut. Kudos, you crazy bastards.

239 Driving would be more interesting if we could all turn left on red, too.

240 It really seems that the voice-over instructions cell phone companies employ are stretched out purposely in order to make you use an extra minute or two on each call. Really, how much instruction does one need for the procedure to disconnect?

241 Have you ever spent an entire car ride surfing the radio dial in frustrating futility just to find a single decent song; then, out of the principle of the thing, continued your search even after you've reached the parking lot of your destination? No? Me neither.

ಬಿಂಚ

242 Even though we're stuck between New York, Massachusetts and Rhode Island, the area surrounding my hometown of Hartford, Connecticut is one of the few in the United States that has little to no discernable regional accent. I'll now demonstrate by reading this Random Thought aloud. Ok. There you are. See? None.

ಬಿಂಚ

243 It's amazing that the health of so many people is negatively impacted by their doctor's poor handwriting. Maybe it's time we had a telethon for this; perhaps get Jerry Lewis a chalkboard to teach calligraphy. Of the many health pitfalls we all have to navigate around daily, penmanship ought to be much further down on the list.

ಬಿಂಚ

244 Yankee Candle ought to come out with a Burnt Popcorn scent. That way, corporate workers can feel more like they're at the office from the comfort of their own homes.

245 Someday, make a quick list of all the things we didn't have as late as the 1970's, yet couldn't live without now. If you're not flabbergasted, you didn't think hard enough.

246 As it turns out, you can actually have more than one "bane of your existence."

247 Watching a basketball game is as boring to me as watching non- contact competitive knitting.

248 Admit it-most of you have occasionally forgotten all about the 'n' in Badminton. It's ok. It happens.

249 Whoever created contractions knew the perfect point at which to deviate from simply slamming two words together to form a similar one, when they went with won't. Willn't just wouldn't have worked.

❧☙

250 I do have to say that 3-D TV is pretty amazing. So it seems the next step, technologically speaking, is being able to actually watch actors perform in real time. They could call it something like a "Play." Maybe have sets, costume changes, perhaps even…oh, right. Well, I guess this is what some might call "coming full circle."

❧☙

251 It seems the only qualification necessary to become an advice columnist is the ability to recommend therapy for virtually any issue. "Dear Twist & Shouting: You're not alone. The inability to separate both halves of an Oreo without breaking the crème filling is the fastest growing cookie affliction in the United States. Oreo Separation Anxiety should not be left untreated. Please, contact 1-844-SEP-CREME for assistance in finding your local OSA meeting place. Good luck."

❧☙

252 If only Achilles had thought to wear high tops that day.

253 Authors who know how to write a great story yet, for some reason, can't write a decent ending, should be able to bring in a 'Literary Closer'-type person. Maybe hire a specialist who'd act like the Mariano Rivera of ending writers. And they shouldn't feel bad about it; columnists don't write their own headlines.

254 Incredible Historical Fact, Part 1: Before becoming head of the Confederate Army, General Robert E. Lee turned down Abraham Lincoln's offer to lead the Union Army. Come on, you know that's a cool fact. Admit it; history can be fun.

255 Incredible Historical Fact, Part II: John Adams and Thomas Jefferson, our 2nd and 3rd presidents, American Revolutionaries, and co-authors of the Declaration of Independence, both died on the same day-July 4, 1826-the 50th Anniversary of our Declaration. Oh, and the US president on that date? John Quincy Adams. Just ponder all of that for a second; I'll wait.

256 Beer may be the only beverage served in a glass that I've never seen anyone drink with a straw.

257 Key chains make surprisingly easy, convenient Christmas tree ornaments.

ଚ୍ଚଓ

258 I'm a Cath-nostic, (Catholic agnostic) who has always thought of religions, collectively, as various tributaries leading to the same river. So I've never understood why people spend so much time caring about how, if, or who other people worship. Chances are we're all wrong about the details, anyway.

ଚ୍ଚଓ

259 The irony of death is that it would be easier if we knew when it was coming; yet, if given the opportunity to know, most would decline the information.

ଚ୍ଚଓ

260 I really think that every new sports stadium should be named after some randomly chosen taxpayer.

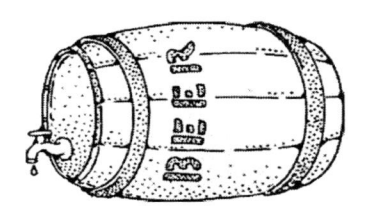

261 We all have our iPods, HDTV and internet. Yet none of the aforementioned could ever surpass the reading of a good book.

ಬಂಡ

262 I know that while bicycling you're supposed to ride with the traffic instead of against it. However, I'd rather trust myself to get out of the way of what I can see; instead of hoping that the coffee slurping, text messaging, newspaper reading guy behind me looks up in time.

ಬಂಡ

263 Apparently, the only thing you need to get rich quick is the ability to convince others that you actually possess the knowledge of how to get rich quick. Also, that you'd be willing to share that knowledge with them for merely the cost of your books, DVD's, and seminars.

ಬಂಡ

264 It intrigues me that with all of its state of the art radar and defense systems, no one on the Death Star was able to detect the Millennium Falcon swooping in at the last second to knock Darth Vader off course.

265 I'm not a Lithuanian on TV, but I do play one in real life.

266 I've never met one man who would have rather been Bill Gates than Hugh Hefner. Not one.

267 Why is playing Solitaire with a deck of cards so boring; yet so addictive when you play it on your computer?

268 How long before we have to start buying electronic stamps for e-mail? Don't tell me that you haven't thought about that.

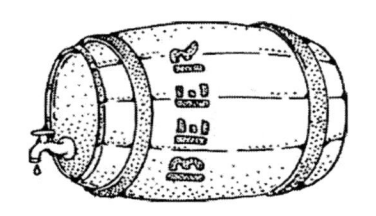

269   I wonder if, when he attends his high school reunions, Superman is tempted to go as himself instead of Clark Kent, just to stick it to the girls that turned him down for the prom.

270   Remember when they used to sell compilation albums of popular TV theme songs of the past? I'm guessing if K-Tel tries to do it again in 20 years, they're going to find their options somewhat limited.

271   If you're going to hold down the same job for 30 years, you probably couldn't do much better than Vanna White's.

272   Have you noticed that the batteries inside some of the newer smart phones evidently have the lifespan of an elderly fruit fly?

273 Whoever said that "nothing is impossible," never tried looking directly at a stop sign while purposely trying not to read it.

274 Did Lemon sharks draw the short straw for names? Though they're dangerous too, I'm guessing that the Great White, Tiger and Bull sharks hang around the water cooler and mock them mercilessly. "Oh, no boys! Quick, let's get out of here; the Lemons are coming!" and then just laugh their asses off.

275 I'm getting so close to winning the lottery; the last few times I've missed it by just 6 numbers.

276 The bagel guillotine is among the most useful yet simplistic gadgets ever created. It's so easy to get carried away with, though. Note to self: bagels, yes; jelly doughnuts, no.

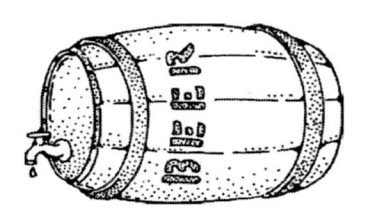

277 I wonder if the devil feels anything like the Washington Generals, the perpetual opponent of the Harlem Globetrotters. Always lining up to play against an old adversary whom he can never beat.

278 When parents name their daughter Sara(h), I'm curious as to what the deciding factor is in adding on-or leaving off- the 'H'.

279 Add me to the scores of people who've never really been that big a fan of clowns. To be fair however, I totally respect any clown who is not that big a fan of writers.

280 Sometimes I wonder why certain pro sports teams, who already had a perfectly fine logo going for them, feel the need to change it to something that looks like it was drawn by Helen Keller on a particularly uninspired day.

281   I'm a jock; but I have to admit that for whatever reason I really love the sound of someone tap dancing.

282   Catching the scent of a wood burning stove as you walk through your neighborhood on a snowy winter's night truly is one of the great, underrated benefits of life.

283   Pet Peeve: People who drag those lunch box-sized suitcases on wheels across the pavement-thereby subjecting you to that 'nails on chalkboard' sound- for a half mile through the parking lot. Pick it up, for the love of (Please insert the Deity of your personal preference, if applicable).

284   Wouldn't Pac Man have been a great spokesman for *Tums*?

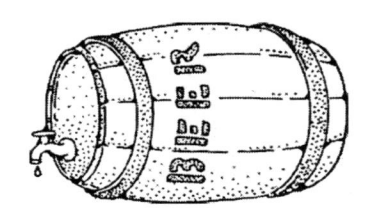

285 Can you imagine a toy company trying to market Lawn Jarts in this era of litigation? Maybe something like, "They can be hours of fun, or else hours of pain. It all really depends, on how good is your aim!"

286 Why is it that when you feel something odd on one side of your body, you immediately check to make sure it's in the same place on the other side, too?

287 If I watch TV for a thousand more years and never hear some character utter the phrase, "the press is gonna have a field day with this," it'll be much, much too soon.

288 A lot of southpaws seem to be nicknamed Lefty; yet for some reason you rarely hear of any northpaws called Righty.

Shouldn't Ice Cold Beer Be Frozen?

289 I once saw a front page newspaper headline touting a study that showed drinking orange juice after brushing your teeth could make the OJ taste bitter. And we all laughed at the guy on those TV spots in that Riddler jacket who screamed the government will give you money for anything.

ಬಿಂಚ

290 That Estelle Getty was in reality the second youngest Golden Girl, younger even than Bea Arthur who played her daughter, still messes with me.

ಬಿಂಚ

291 That high school class I took on how to use an electric typewriter is beginning to seem more and more like a huge waste of time.

ಬಿಂಚ

292 Pet Peeve: Companies that have no problem calling you at home or sending you their junk mail, yet have the nerve to post signs on their brick and mortar buildings that read *No Soliciting*.

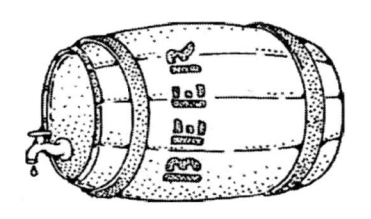

293   Though the movie *Wargames* was awesome, I'm sorry to tell you Joshua that Tic-Tac-Toe can be won; you just have to start in the corners. One can only hope that the next time a computer learning a game is the only way to avert a nuclear war, it's not that simpleton 1983 version with the Pong-esque graphics.

294   Q and U are kind of like the Siamese twins of the alphabet.

295   On the one hand, it would be cool if urinals could double as slot machines; on the other, no one would ever have a desire to collect the payout.

296   It seems that when I mail a bill, the check I wrote clears almost before the envelope hits the bottom of the mailbox. Yet when I'm depositing into my personal account, there's like a ten year hold on the check.

297   I'll never understand how an aircraft carrier can float across the ocean, while a penny will sink straight to the bottom.

298   It must be pretty hard for even a white collar beaver to get decent dental coverage.

299   I wonder if the many companies who shed employees for technological replacements will take a moment to consider who will have the money to pay for their products, once the majority of the country no longer has a job.

300   Plastic Man just doesn't sound like the right name for him. Rubber Man seems more appropriate. Plus he could really clean up in endorsements pitching prophylactics; maybe even literally become Trojan Man.

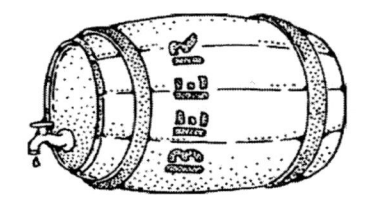

301 Why is it that even if your freezer is filled to the brim with ice cream, you'll still sprint after the Good Humor truck if it drives through your neighborhood?

ಶುಲ್

302 I'm a little tired of hearing that iceberg lettuce is the junk food of lettuce. Sure, it's solidified green water. That doesn't make it a double cheeseburger, though.

ಶುಲ್

303 Pet Peeve: When someone gives you his or her absurdly common surname and then feels compelled to spell it slowly for you. "That's Dan Jones. J-O-N-E-S." Even better is when they have an impossible first name, but spell only the last. "I'm Jehosephat Xanadu Smith. S-M-I-T-H."

ಶುಲ್

304 Caller ID eradicates Telephone Roulette, and with it strips away one of life's few remaining innocent Leaps of Faith. Remember this? Brrrring! "There's the phone. It's probably either that hot girl I just met, or the electric company about that overdue bill. "Hello? Damn. Electric company."

305 At a sporting event when a ball or puck goes into the stands and is snagged by some middle-aged guy, the fans start chanting "Give it to the kid," if there's one nearby. Why? This guy's been waiting 40 years for that moment and now he's got to give it up to someone who has decades in front of him to get his own? To that guy I say, "Keep it, adult."

306 I loved that ABC's *Schoolhouse Rock!* could summarize the entire American Revolution in one catchy 3 minute cartoon music video.

307 It's sad watching people on the Family Feud having to clap for the breathtakingly stupid answers one of their clan gives. You've seen it-Host: "Name something you put on toast." Contestant: "Cream of Wheat?" Rest of Family: "Good answer!!!" Surrrrvey, says: Moron.

308 I'd be interested in knowing the final statistical results of that *Just Say No* campaign from the 1980's.

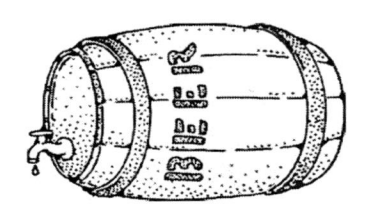

309   Crossword puzzles would be harder to create if their writers had to use apostrophes where appropriate.

ଔଓ

310   I know hindsight is 20/20; but as you are now completely certain about what has already occurred, shouldn't it be more like 20/15?

ଔଓ

311   I wonder how British General Charles Cornwallis would feel today if he could see that massive bridge spanning the York River; connecting Yorktown, Virginia to Gloucester Point. I guess timing really is everything.

ଔଓ

312   So if I've got this right: honey is good forever, but bottled water has an expiration date?

313 To those too afraid to give an oral presentation in a class setting, fear not. Your audience is either thinking about what they're going to say on their turn, or totally tuning you out. Unless, of course, you're hot. And in that case, technically, they're still tuning you out. There you are. No charge.

ಲ‍ಜ

314 Why is it that nobody ever seems offended by Notre Dame's Fighting Irish mascot?

ಲ‍ಜ

315 If Thomas Paine were to write Common Sense today, he'd be over 250 years old. Just kidding, I couldn't resist. Let's try that one again. If Thomas Paine wrote Common Sense today, he'd be lucky to sell 4 copies.

ಲ‍ಜ

316 How come when my credit card tries to upsell me on a new feature, the correspondence comes with a convenient, postage paid envelope. Yet when I get their normal bill I'd damn well better have a stamp on me?

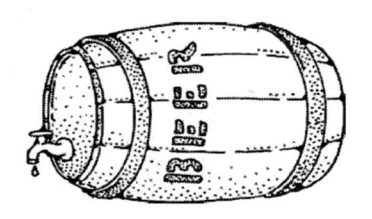

317   What were the odds that nearly half the main cast of the movie *Predator* would go on to become United States governors?

318   Sure, a broken clock is right twice a day; but if it's your only clock how would you know when that was?

319   C'mon, now. If you had taken the SAT's with a #3 lead pencil, would it really have made any difference?

320   As a grammar school student standing in cold weather at bus stops as recently as the mid-1980's, I certainly don't recall this phenomenon of school buses delaying thousands of automobile commuters daily by driving forty feet at a time before stopping at each passenger's house individually.

Shouldn't Ice Cold Beer Be Frozen?

321 It's interesting how many people in the receiving line at a wake will say of the deceased, "He's in a better place now;" yet not one of them would be willing to take his place in the casket.

322 Saying "I know this sounds cliché" prior to making your statement is, in and of itself, a cliché.

323 One thing that The Man can never take away from us is that we can spell *Chanukah* and *Catsup* any of two different ways each, and still be correct.

324 I don't care how strong *Crazy Glue* claims to be; it's significantly doubtful that I'd ever hang mid-air from the steel beam of a skyscraper while holding on to nothing more than a hardhat that they glued to it. Look, I'm sure it's a fine glue, but I think I'll just take their word for it.

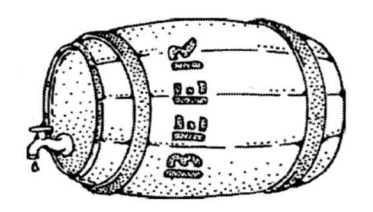

325   If God won't stop a tsunami from crashing into an island, what makes some people think He'll take a little time out of His day to pop in and help their team's guy kick a game winning field goal?

326   Don't kid yourself; leftover pizza is much better cold than reheated.

327   The world would be a little better place if more stuff came covered in bubble wrap.

328   Why did Alvin get first billing? Simon and Theodore obviously put more effort into the songs

Shouldn't Ice Cold Beer Be Frozen?

329 When you think about it, 704 really ought to be the area code for Philadelphia, Pennsylvania.

ଝଓ

330 Do you think the Wonder Twins were the laughing stock of the Hall of Justice? I can just imagine Batman in the breakroom laughing with The Green Lantern and Aquaman at Zan and Jayna, while they hang around all day waiting for that one call requesting an orangutan carrying a bucket of water.

ଝଓ

331 While I'm certain that there's some sort of unfounded grammatical rule that technically allows it, why are they called Men's rooms when the word men itself is already plural?

ଝଓ

332 Pet Peeve: Waiting at a stop light that has a built in green left turn arrow that never lights up; causing you to wait forever for the line of oncoming cars to pass. I mean, what's the point of installing it if it doesn't get used?

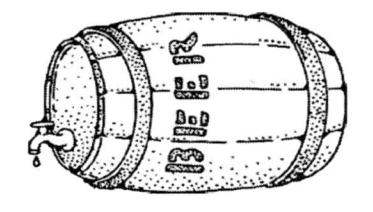

333   Yes, the commercials insist; but how do you really know what brand of food a dog thinks tastes better? "Hello folks, Fido here. Listen, take it from me. Nothing hits the spot better after a long day of chasing cars and digging up lawns than a nice can of Alpo."

334   When you think about it, there really shouldn't have been more than one *World's Greatest Grandpa* mug ever made. At least at a time.

335   Here's some free advice to the 75% or so who've ever posted in an online forum and used the nonexistent insult "looser" while responding to other posters: Fyi, it's spelled "loser." Although you do have to admire the irony.

336   You don't see many female juniors. You know, like: "Hi, nice to meet you. I'm Mary Smith, Jr."

Shouldn't Ice Cold Beer Be Frozen?

337 Admit it-when you come across the wedding notices in the newspaper, you check to see if the guy's fiancée is too good looking for him; and also to compare if their looks ratio is better than the one between you and your own girlfriend.

ഌഃ

338 Twenty years ago I was completely enthralled with having a beeper. Now, I get irked if it takes more than ten seconds for my cell phone to text a picture to my friend in California.

ഌഃ

339 I've always thought that with their Munchkins, Dunkin' Donuts would make a great sole sponsor of the annual *Wizard of Oz* broadcast; the same way York Peppermint Patties used to sponsor the Charlie Brown specials.

ഌഃ

340 The 5th biggest thing I'm going to miss when I'm dead is a wicked cold glass of ice water on a sweltering summer day. (And yes, smart alec, I am aware that ice cold water should also be frozen)

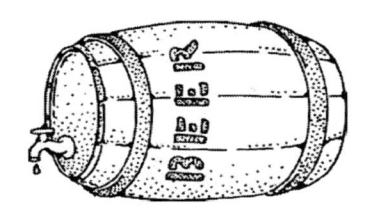

341 Have you ever done a word search and found a word that wasn't on the list provided at the bottom? You really should still get credit for that.

ಬಐ

342 Do you know what would be great? If microwave popcorn bags came with individual sized packets of dental floss.

ಬಐ

343 Pet Peeve: Whipped cream frosting on birthday cakes. Damn it, people- if you're going to eat cake; eat cake.

ಬಐ

344 Did Buzz Aldrin lose a coin flip to Neil Armstrong regarding who would step out of the lunar module first? I think I'd at least bring it up. "Whoa, Neil. Hold up there a sec, Big Fella. You think you can jump out first just 'cause you've got the 'money quote'?" At the very least I'd insist on Paper, Rock and Scissors.

345   Why does any psychic need to work for a living? They can't all be philanthropists.

346   Why do women's health club locker rooms have wondrous amenities and individual, aesthetically beautiful shower stalls; while men get 12 shower spigots sticking out of the wall in a glorified closet; just like in high school gym class?

347   Remember those walkie-talkies they sold us kids in the 1980's that had the ability to use Morse code? Although no one I knew ever got past learning how to type S-O-S, it was good to know that if we ever fell into a well and a World War II naval officer happened by, that knowledge would've paid off huge.

348   Ever wonder if the people who use the word boast, when brag would suffice, are also the same type of people who would substitute feasible for possible while engaging in everyday conversation? Their esoteric reasoning is beyond an obtuse simpleton like me.

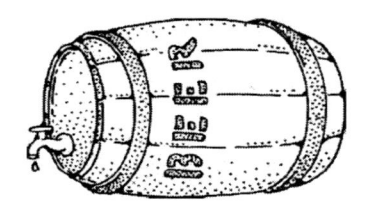

349 As you're falling asleep and begin to dream, why don't you ever see those wavy, transitional lines like you do every time a TV sitcom character nods off?

ಬಂಡ

350 It's pretty cool how that watery liquid hand soap magically turns foamy as soon as you pump it out.

ಬಂಡ

351 It really seems as if cereal boxes just don't come with prizes in the bottom anymore. I mean what else is baking soda for; if not to make those little plastic tub submarines float?

ಬಂಡ

352 Throughout television history there have been many implausible concepts; the most improbable of which has got to be *I Dream of Jeannie*. Tony Nelson lives with a gorgeous, endlessly wish-granting genie who falls completely in love with him; yet he elects to keep her at a distance while instead making sure she doesn't cost him his job? Not. Buying. It.

353 Did you ever hear someone utter the phrase, "this joke writes itself"? Well, here's one that does, literally. The following is from a placard in a doctor's office, verbatim: "According to the National Highway Traffic Safety Administration, visibility is one of the basic requirements for safe driving." Admittedly, they're right. It sure is.

೮౧

354 Somewhere in New England there's an invisible line where people living north of it refer to soda as "pop," for some reason. All that I'm certain of is that Connecticut is south of that line.

೮౧

355 Why does it seem that in every movie or TV show featuring a character walking home from a grocery store, he or she always seems to be carrying a brown bag that has unwrapped celery stalks sticking out?

೮౧

356 Hi! Let's play a word game. Which one of the following does not belong in this group: Ready? 1. Hades 2. Hell 3. Perdition 4. An Office Cubicle. Give up? The answer is: There is absolutely no difference whatsoever between them. Sorry, this was a trick question.

357   I've become convinced that the Pilgrims bypassed Connecticut to land in Massachusetts simply because they were not prepared to tolerate the absurdly restrictive beer laws we have here.

358   It's nice that some GPS systems come with the option to use a British accent, though I think it'd be cool if they came with some others, too. Maybe Southern Belle; or even California Surfer, so you could hear instructions such as "In, like, four hundred feet take a right, Dude."

359   There ought to be a strict law created and enforced against people who, though they have no intention whatsoever of crossing the street, still hit the *Push to Cross* button at intersections anyway as they walk by.

360   I was once asked why, since they had both come to prominence in 1880's London, Sherlock Holmes never tried to catch Jack the Ripper? You might think that inanity of this magnitude would be relatively uncommon, though I've discovered that in reality no, it really isn't.

Shouldn't Ice Cold Beer Be Frozen?

361 Have you ever finally gotten around to watching your first episode of a popular, long-running TV show; then six months later you go to watch it again and it's that same episode you'd already seen?

෨෬

362 What's the appropriate distance to slow down when you're far enough behind someone who you think will hold the door open for you- yet you'd rather they not- simply because you don't want to have to respect their courtesy by sprinting for the door?

෨෬

363 With all due respect to Kevin Bacon; you could probably play instead the 1 Degree of Donald Sutherland. The man has acted in so many productions; I could probably connect him to myself just from *The Ghost of the Christmas Ships* play I was in back in 6th Grade.

෨෬

364 If, with less than two outs, there are runners at first and second base, or the bases are loaded, and the batter hits a pop-up judged by the umpire to be catchable without extraordinary exertion, that batter is called out at once; regardless of whether the ball is subsequently caught. Runners are free to advance the bases at their own risk. See? Contrary to what you may have heard, the Infield Fly rule isn't all that difficult to grasp.

Chris Gay

365 No one lives their life vicariously through me. At least not yet.

Afterword

Hey, you made it. Good for you. Oh, and if you're meaning to ask me why there aren't 366 Random Thoughts to account for Leap Years, I guess that's fair enough. I'll tell you what; we'll compromise. Here's ¼ of a Random Thought: "Get a l…" With that said, I hope you've enjoyed the various takes on life by this unapologetic Generation X'er. And you thought that we were all just a bunch of apathetic, self-centered, video gaming, apolitical drifters who get our news from late night TV monologues. Well, let me just tell you right here and now-I rarely play video games.

Speaking of shameless plugs, for more of my writings visit:

my website, www.thepassionofthechris.com

my blog , chrisgay.wordpress.com